Steven Spielberg

By Wil Mara

Consultant
Nanci R. Vargus, Ed.D.
Assistant Professor of Literacy
University of Indianapolis, Indianapolis, Indiana

New York   Sydney
                                                   g
Danbury, Connecticut

Designer: Herman Adler Design
Photo Researcher: Caroline Anderson
The photo on the cover shows Steven Spielberg.

Library of Congress Cataloging-in-Publication Data

Mara, Wil.
  Steven Spielberg / by Wil Mara.
     p. cm. — (Rookie biographies)
  Includes index.
  ISBN 0-516-21842-5 (lib. bdg.)   0-516-25821-4 (pbk.)
  1. Spielberg, Steven—Juvenile literature. 2. Motion picture producers and
directors—United States—Biography—Juvenile literature. I. Title. II. Rookie
biography
  PN1998.3.S65M27 2005
  791.4302'33'092—dc22

                              2004015315

Lights! Camera! Action!
Have you ever wanted to
make a movie?

These people are making a movie.

4

Steven Spielberg did. He has always loved movies.

He wanted to spend his life making them!

Spielberg was born in Ohio in 1946. He saw his first movie at age six.

Spielberg began making his own movies. He used his father's camera. His family and friends were the actors.

Spielberg is standing behind the camera.

Spielberg used toy trains, like this one, in his movies.

Spielberg also used his toy trains to make movies about train wrecks (REKS).

He won a prize for a movie he made when he was 13. One of his movies was shown in a real theater when he was 16.

D i e j o

Spielberg thought about making movies all of the time.

One day he went to a movie studio. He found an empty closet and used it as his office.

These people are watching a movie being made at a studio.

Spielberg visited Universal Studios in California.

Spielberg did not have a job at the studio. He went there everyday anyway. While there, he made a movie!

Important people at the studio saw Spielberg's movie. They decided to give him a job.

The studio asked Spielberg to be a director (duh-RECK-tuhr). A director tells actors what to do.

Spielberg was 20 years old. He was the youngest person ever to be a director.

15

This is a poster for the movie *Duel*.

At first, Spielberg directed television shows. But, he really wanted to direct movies.

So, Spielberg made a movie for television called *Duel* (DOO-uhl).

It was a hit! People loved the movie.

Spielberg's first chance to direct a movie for theaters finally came. He directed a scary movie about sharks. It was called *Jaws*.

Millions of people watched it. After seeing the movie, many people were afraid to go to the beach.

Spielberg talks to the actors from *Jaws*. This is Spielberg.

This is a picture from *Close Encounters of the Third Kind.*

Spielberg's next movie was called *Close Encounters of the Third Kind.*

It was about space beings who come to Earth from another planet. People loved this movie, too.

Have you seen the movie *E. T.*?

This is a picture from *E. T. The Extra-Terrestrial.*

Did you scream when you saw the giant dinosaurs in *Jurassic Park*? Spielberg made these movies, too.

Spielberg has made many famous movies.

Spielberg's movies can make you scream or cry. Other times they make you laugh.

Raiders of the Lost Ark was another movie Spielberg made.

This is Spielberg and his wife, Kate Capshaw.

Spielberg says his family makes him happy. He and his wife have seven children.

Steven Spielberg is a great movie director. He will make many more wonderful movies.

What about you? Will you make a movie one day?

29

Words You Know

camera

dinosaur

Steven Spielberg

studio

toy train

31

Index

About the Author

More than fifty published books bear Wil Mara's name. He has written both fiction and nonfiction, for both children and adults. He lives with his family in northern New Jersey. He enjoys watching Steven Spielberg movies.

Photo Credits

5/12 ⑧
8/14 ⑩